Dear Friend,

Handmade happiness is just a few stitches away! That's because the Country Friends have gathered their favorite ideas for making thoughtful gifts and accessories and put them all in *Sew Simple*, a collection of 20 designs you'll love to create. And because most of these projects are quick & easy, they're perfect for beginners.

Whip up an apron from a handed-down tablecloth. Create covered hangers, a set of coasters or a pot holder in your favorite retro fabrics. For your friends who knit or crochet, make roll-up holders to store their needles and hooks. You'll also find three yummy recipes to enjoy while you sew…Chewy Chocolate-Caramel Bars, Creamy Morning Coffee and Tickled-Pink Drink.

Let these ideas inspire you to dust off your sewing machine or get out your needle and thread. You'll want to treat your friends…and yourself to the simple pleasure of sweetly-sewn gifts!

Stitch up some fun!

Vickie & Jo Ann

PLACEMATS
Basic Instructions, *pages 36-39*

For each placemat, you will need:
- nine 6"x7½" fabric pieces (we cut ours from four print fabrics)
- 16"x20½" piece of backing fabric
- 16"x20½" piece of interfacing
- 2 yards rickrack
- clear nylon thread

Piece together springy prints, add a little rickrack and you'll have cheery new placemats in no time. Match right sides of the fabric and use a ½" seam allowance for all sewing.

To make each placemat, arrange the fabric pieces in three rows. Sew the pieces together to make one row at a time. **Matching intersections,** sew the rows together to make the front of the placemat. Lay the backing piece right side up on your work surface. Stack the front piece (right side down), then the interfacing on the backing. Leaving an opening for turning, sew the layers together. **Trim the corners,** turn right side out and press. Sew the opening closed. Zigzag rickrack around the edges with nylon thread.

2

CHEWY CHOCOLATE-CARAMEL BARS

You'll be reaching for another one of these!

1 c. quick-cooking oats, uncooked
1 c. all-purpose flour
½ c. brown sugar, packed
½ c. sugar
1 t. baking soda
¾ c. butter, melted
14-oz. pkg. caramels, unwrapped
3 T. milk
12-oz. pkg. milk chocolate chips

Combine oats, flour, brown sugar, sugar, baking soda and butter; press half of mixture into a greased 9"x9" baking dish. Bake at 350 degrees for 10 minutes. While baking, melt caramels with milk in a double boiler; stir until smooth. Sprinkle chocolate chips over hot crust; pour melted caramel on top. Spread remaining dry mixture over top; bake 15 more minutes. Cool; cut into squares. Keep refrigerated. Makes one dozen.

Linda Kohrs
Mesa, AZ

APKINS

sic Instructions, pages 36-39
tterns, page 29

r each napkin, you will need:
1" fabric square
⅓ yards rickrack
lear nylon thread
quid fray preventative
aper-backed fusible web
rint fabric scraps for the bird
and wing
racing paper
mbroidery floss
2" diameter button

Use leftover prints from the placemats to make an adorable chirper to appliqué on each napkin. Press the edges of the fabric square ¼" to the wrong side twice; **hem**. Pin rickrack near the edges and trim the ends; sew using nylon thread. Apply fray preventative to the rickrack ends. Iron fusible web to the back of the fabric scraps. Using the patterns, cut the bird and wing shapes from the fabric. Remove the paper backing and fuse the **appliqués** near one corner of the napkin. Use 3 strands of floss and sew **running stitch** legs and outlines and add **straight stitch** feet. Add the button for the eye.

TABLECLOTH APRON
Basic Instructions, *pages 36-39*

- vintage-look tablecloth
- embroidered hankie
- $^3/_4$" diameter button

This sweet apron made from vintage linens will remind you of Grandma. Use a $^1/_2$" seam allowance for all sewing unless otherwise noted.

For the apron skirt, find a pretty spot on your tablecloth and cut a rectangle the size you want (ours is 17"x28"). Press the short ends and the bottom long edge of the skirt $^1/_4$" to the wrong side twice; **hem**.

For the waistband/tie, cut a 6" strip the length of the tablecloth. (Ours is 72" long…if you'd like yours to be longer than your tablecloth, just cut a waistband strip 1" longer than the apron skirt and two more strips for the ties. Sew them together.) Press the ends and long edges $^1/_2$" to the wrong side. Matching wrong sides and long edges, fold the waistband/tie in half. Center and pin the top of the skirt between the pressed edges of the waistband/tie. Sew along the pressed ends and edges.

Cut a pocket from the tablecloth (we cut ours 7$^1/_2$"x8"). Cut a corner from the hankie to fit on the pocket. Matching the raw edges, layer right sides up and pin the pocket and hankie piece together. Press the top edges $^1/_2$" to the wrong side and **topstitch**. Press the side and bottom edges $^1/_2$" to the wrong side and pin to the apron. Topstitch along the remaining pressed edges. Sew the button to the point of the hankie.

POT HOLDER & COASTERS
Basic Instructions, *pages 36-39*
Project Instructions, page 24

TEA TOWEL APRON
Turn a striped tea towel into an apron in seconds. Just **topstitch** twill tape along one edge of the towel for the waistband/tie…simple!

CREAMY MORNING COFFEE

Even non-coffee folks will like this.

3½ c. milk
¼ c. instant coffee granules
¼ c. brown sugar, packed
⅛ t. salt

Pour milk into a saucepan;
heat until just boiling. Remove
from heat; add remaining
ingredients, stirring to dissolve.
Makes 4 cups.

SUNFLOWER PILLOW

Basic Instructions, pages 36-39
Patterns, page 29

- ⁷/₈ yard solid cotton fabric for pillow front and backing
- paper-backed fusible web and clear nylon thread (optional)
- fat quarter for petals
- fabric scrap for flower center
- tracing paper
- 2 yards jumbo green rickrack
- coordinating colors of embroidery floss
- 14" square pillow form

Kick back and relax with this bright & sunny pillow. Cut a 15" square from solid fabric for the pillow front and two 15"x18" pieces for the pillow backing. Matching the wrong sides and short ends, fold the backing pieces in half and press.

Choose one or both **appliqué** methods. Using the patterns, cut 7 petals and the flower center from the fabric pieces. (We backed the petals with fusible web, but didn't back the flower center since we wanted the edges to fray.) Arrange the petals on the pillow front, trimming them to fit.

Add the flower center and pin a rickrack stem in place. Appliqué the pieces to the pillow front. Use 3 strands of floss and add a **running stitch** to the flower center, petals and stem.

Pin rickrack around the outer edges of the pillow front. Sew along the middle of the rickrack. Matching raw edges and overlapping the pressed ends, pin the folded pillow backing pieces to the right side of the pillow front. Turn the cover over; sew the front to the backing along the previously sewn lines. **Trim the corners** and turn right side out. Insert the pillow form.

O-YO PILLOW

Basic Instructions, *pages 36-39*

/4 yard solid cotton fabric for
pillow front and backing
1/2" diameter circle template
en coordinating 5" fabric squares
coordinating thread or
embroidery floss
en coordinating buttons
clear nylon thread
2"x16" pillow form

This quick & easy pillow will remind you of the yo-yo coverlet on your Great Aunt's guest bed. Cut a 13"x17" piece from solid fabric for the pillow front and two 13"x20" pieces for the pillow backing. Matching the wrong sides and short ends, fold the backing pieces in half and press.

Using the template, cut a 4¹/₂" circle from each 5" square. Make a **yo-yo** from each circle. Sew a button to the center of each yo-yo with thread or floss. Arrange the yo-yos on the pillow front and use nylon thread to sew them in place.

Matching raw edges and overlapping the pressed ends, pin, then sew the folded pillow backing pieces to the right side of the pillow front using a ¹/₂" seam allowance. **Trim the corners** and turn right side out. Insert the pillow form.

STRIP-PIECED PILLOW

Basic Instructions, pages 36-39
Pattern, page 30

- rotary cutter, cutting mat and ruler
- ¼ yard each of three print fabrics
- ⅝ yard of solid cotton fabric
- tracing paper
- felt scrap
- 1½" diameter self-covered button
- 14" square pillow form

Match right sides and use a ¼" seam allowance for all sewing unless otherwise noted.

Pull the colors in your room together with a refreshing accent pillow. Use the **rotary cutter** to cut the print fabrics into 2"x40" strips. Cut two 2"x40" strips and two 15"x18" pillow backing pieces from solid fabric. Matching the wrong sides and short ends, fold the backing pieces in half and press.

Arrange and sew six strips together along the long edges. Press the seam allowances open. Cut four 8" squares from the pieced strips. Arrange the squares, alternating the stripes vertically and horizontally.

Using a ½" seam allowance, sew the squares together in pairs. Sew the pieced squares together.

Using the pattern, cut a scalloped flower from felt. Cover the button with a print fabric scrap. Sew the button and the felt flower to the pillow front.

Matching raw edges and overlapping the pressed ends, pin, then sew the folded pillow backing pieces to the right side of the pillow front using a ½" seam allowance. **Trim the corners** and turn right side out. Insert the pillow form.

OVERED HANGERS

asic Instructions, pages 36-39
oject Instructions, page 26

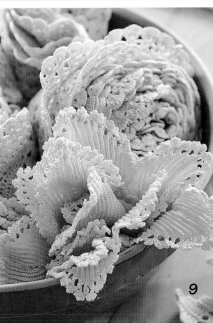

GIFT BAGS

Basic Instructions, pages 36-39
Pattern, page 33

For each bag, you will need:
- tea towel, napkin or fabric piece
- fabric glue
- mini rickrack
- rub-on initial
- clothespin
- tracing paper
- water-soluble fabric marker
- two 5" fabric squares
  (we used a print and a solid)
- pinking shears
- felt scrap
- 1/2" to 5/8" diameter button

Perfect for giving favors or special thank-you's. Using an existing hem for the top (long edge) of the bag, cut a 6³/4"x8¹/2" piece from a tea towel or napkin. (If you wish to make yours from a piece of fabric, cut the piece 7¹/4"x8¹/2" and press one long edge ¹/4" to the wrong side twice; **hem**.)

Matching the right sides and short edges, fold the fabric in half. Sew along the side and bottom edges and turn right side out. Glue rickrack around the top of the bag.

To make the clip-on flower, apply the rub-on to the end of the clothespin. Trace the petal pattern onto tracing paper and cut out. Use the fabric marker and draw around the pattern to make five petals on one fabric square, leaving ¹/2" between petals. Matching the wrong sides, pin the squares together and sew along the drawn lines. Use pinking shears to cut out the petals ¹/8" larger than the stitching lines and to cut two 1" diameter felt circles. Fold the point of the petals into a pleat and glue them between the felt circles. Sew the button to the front of the flower through all layers. Glue the flower to the clothespin.

10

DRAWSTRING BAG
Basic Instructions, pages 36-39
Project Instructions, page 27

JEWELRY POUCH
Basic Instructions, pages 36-39

- ¼ yard print fabric
- vintage-look hankies and fabric scraps
- assorted trims (we used rickrack, lace and crocheted edgings)
- scallop-edged scissors
- buttons

Old fabric scraps conjure up good memories…turn your favorites into this sweet jewelry pouch. Cut two 8"x16" fabric pieces for the pouch and lining. Arrange and pin pieces cut from hankies and fabric scraps on the pouch fabric. Trim the pieces to fit. Cover the raw edges of some of the pieces with trims. **Topstitch** the pieces and trims to the pouch fabric, using straight or zigzag stitches.

Matching right sides and straight edges, sew an 8" trim length to one short end of the pouch fabric for the edge of the flap (we sewed crocheted trim to ours). Matching the right sides and using a ½" seam allowance, sew the lining to the pouch along the short ends. Turn right side out and press.

For the pocket, fold the end opposite the flap 6" to the wrong side. Using a ¼" seam allowance, sew along the long edges of the pouch, securing the pocket. Scallop the edges, being careful not to clip the stitching.

Sew buttons to the pouch as desired.

SLING BAG
Basic Instructions, pages 36-39
Project Instructions, pages 24-25

CROCHET HOOK ROLL
Basic Instructions, *pages 36-39*

- 19½"x25" fabric piece for the body
- 12"x19½" fabric piece for the pocket
- 1½" wide twill tape
- ½" wide vintage edging
- clear nylon thread
- 12½"x19½" piece of batting
- ¾" wide jumbo rickrack
- two 1½" tall D rings
- liquid fray preventative (optional)

If you're hooked on crochet, this small-size roll is just right for you. Match right sides and use a ½" seam allowance for all sewing unless otherwise noted.

Matching the wrong sides and short ends, fold the body in half. Matching the wrong sides and long edges, fold the pocket in half. Press the folds.

Cut a 19½" length each from twill tape and edging. Layer and pin the trims near the fold of the pocket; zigzag with nylon thread.

Unfold the body wrong side up. Pin, then baste the batting to the lower half of the fabric, aligning one long edge of the batting with the fold. Leaving the piece unfolded, turn the body right side up, with the basting on the lower half. Aligning the raw edges, place the folded pocket on the lower half of the body and place rickrack ⅛" from the bottom edge; pin, then baste along the side and bottom edges. Matching right sides and short edges, fold the body in half. Leaving an opening on one side for turning, sew the sides and bottom together through all thicknesses. Turn right side out and press. Sew the opening closed. **Topstitch** around the crochet hook roll ¼" from the edges.

Pin, then sew every 4½" from top to bottom to divide the pockets into sections.

Cut a 12" length of twill tape for the closure. Press one end ¼" to the wrong side twice; **hem.** Thread the hemmed end through the D rings, fold, then sew across the tape to hold the rings in place. Sew the tape to the back of the roll as shown (Fig. 1).

Fig. 1

Trim the tape end and apply fray preventative if desired. Place the hooks in the pockets, fold the top down and roll up to fasten.

TICKLED-PINK DRINK
A yummy strawberry drink.

10-oz. pkg. frozen strawberries, thawed
1 c. orange juice
½ c. milk
½ c. vanilla yogurt
1 t. almond extract
Garnish: one orange, sliced into thin wedges

Place all ingredients except orange wedges into a blender; cover and blend until smooth, 40 to 50 seconds. Pour into serving glasses; garnish each with an orange wedge. Makes 3½ cups.

KNITTING NEEDLE ROLL
Basic Instructions, pages 36-39

- 21"x34" fabric piece for the body
- 21"x24" fabric piece for the top pocket
- 17"x21" fabric piece for the bottom pocket
- $3/8$" and $5/8$" wide ribbon
- clear nylon thread
- 21"x16$1/2$" piece of batting
- 1$1/4$" wide twill tape
- large sewing snap
- large button

You'll want to carry this wonderful roll everywhere…you'll always be ready to start a new project. Match right sides and use a $1/2$" seam allowance for all sewing unless otherwise noted.

Matching the wrong sides and short ends, fold the body and top pocket in half. Matching the wrong sides and long edges, fold the bottom pocket in half. Press the folds.

Cut a 21" length from each ribbon. Pin the ribbons near the folds of the pockets; zigzag with nylon thread.

Unfold the body wrong side up. Pin, then baste the batting to the lower half of the fabric, aligning one long edge of the batting with the fold. Leaving the piece unfolded, turn the body right side up, with the basting on the lower half. Aligning raw edges, layer the folded top and bottom pockets on the lower half of the body; pin, then baste along the side and bottom edges. Matching right sides and short ends, fold the body in half. Leaving an opening at the bottom for turning, sew the sides and bottom together through thicknesses. Turn right side out and press. Sew the opening closed. **Topstitch** around the needle roll $1/2$" from the edges.

Pin, then sew every 4$3/4$" from top to bottom to divide the pockets into sections.

Cut a 12" length of twill tape for the closure. Press the ends $1/4$" to the wrong side twice; **hem** each end. Sew one end to the back of the needle roll at the center of one short edge. Sew half of the snap to this end of the tape. Sew the other half to the wrong side and the button to the right side of the other tape end.

Just add knitting needles and you're ready to roll.

TOTE BAG
Basic Instructions, pages 36-39

- 21"x25" and 21"x28" pieces of lightweight interfacing
- 21"x25" piece of tote fabric
- 21"x28" piece of lining fabric
- 2⁷/₈ yards of 1¹/₄" wide twill tape
- two 1" diameter buttons

Take this summery tote on all your adventures. Match right sides and use a ¹/₂" seam allowance for all sewing unless otherwise noted.

Baste the interfacing pieces to the wrong side of the tote and lining pieces. Turn the tote piece right side up.

Beginning where shown (Fig. 1), pin twill tape to the tote piece, allowing for a 24" handle loop at each end of the tote. Overlapping the tape ends, fold the top end under ¹/₂" (trim if needed) and pin in place. **Topstitch** the tape to the tote piece along each long edge of the tape, stopping and starting 1" from the edges of the tote fabric.

Fig. 1

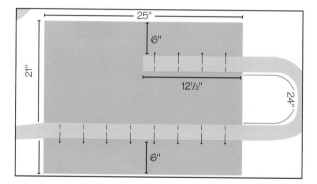

Matching the right sides and short ends, fold the tote piece in half. Sew the sides together. To form the bottom corners, match the side seams to the bottom fold. Sew across each corner ³/₄" from the point (Fig. 2). Turn the tote right side out.

Fig. 2

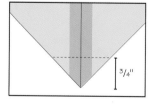

Repeat to sew the lining sides together and to form the bottom corners; do not turn right side out. Place the tote inside the lining and pin the top edges together. Leaving an opening for turning, sew along the top edges, being careful not to catch the handles in the stitching. Turn right side out and press (about ³/₄" of the lining will show above the top edge of the tote).

Topstitch just below the top edge of the tote fabric, catching the handles in the stitching. Sew buttons to the tote front.

18

BOY'S RECEIVING BLANKET
Basic Instructions, pages 36-39
Patterns, page 31

- 36" cotton fabric square
- 4¼ yards of ³/₈" wide twill tape
- clear nylon thread
- paper-backed fusible web
- fabric scraps
- white thread

The zigzagged edges on the truck appliqué make this blanket baby-boy tough. Press the edges of the background fabric square ½" to the right side, **mitering** the corners. Pin the twill tape trim to the fabric, covering the raw edges and **mitering** the corners. **Topstitch** along the long edges of the tape using nylon thread.

Use the fusible web **appliqué** method and cut a truck, window and wheels from fabric scraps. Fuse the pieces to the blanket and zigzag around the edges with nylon thread. Sew an X in the center of each wheel using 2 strands of white thread.

GIRL'S RECEIVING BLANKET
Basic Instructions, *pages 36-39*
Patterns, *page 30*

- 36" cotton fabric square
- 4 yards jumbo rickrack
- clear nylon thread
- paper-backed fusible web
- fabric scraps

Press the edges of the background fabric square ½" to the right side. Pin the rickrack to the fabric, covering the raw edges. Using nylon thread, zigzag the rickrack in place.

Use the fusible web **appliqué** method and cut a flower and flower center from fabric scraps. Fuse the pieces to the blanket and zigzag around the edges with nylon thread.

21

APPLIQUÉD BABY BLANKET

Basic Instructions, pages 36-39
Patterns, pages 30, 32 and 33

- 40" cotton fabric square for blanket front
- 40" cotton fabric square for backing
- paper-backed fusible web or tracing paper
- fabric scraps for flowers and leaves
- assorted green trims for stems
- clear nylon thread
- coordinating embroidery floss
- 4¹/₂ yards jumbo rickrack for edging

Give your appliqués soft, frayed edges like we did, or use fusible web to give the flowers a smooth, finished look…pick the style you like best! Match right sides and use a ¹/₂" seam allowance for all sewing unless otherwise noted.

Leaving an opening for turning, sew the blanket fabric and backing together. Turn right side out and press. Sew the opening closed.

Choose an **appliqué** method and cut the flower and leaf appliqués from fabric scraps. Arrange the flowers, leaves and stems and appliqué them to the blanket front (we zigzagged along the middle of the stems with nylon thread).

Using six strands of floss, sew a **running stitch** around the leaves and flowers. For a sweet finished edge, sew rickrack along the outer edges of the blanket.

RIBBIT
Basic Instructions, pages 36-39
Project Instructions, page 28

DON'T JUDGE EACH DAY BY THE HARVEST YOU REAP BUT BY THE SEEDS YOU PLANT. ~ROBERT LOUIS STEVENSON

POT HOLDER & COASTERS
Basic Instructions, *pages 36-39*
(also shown on page 5)

- rotary cutter, cutting mat and ruler
- 18" wide solid and print fabric scraps (we chose 2 solids and 5 prints)
- 1/4 yard backing fabric
- batting
- clear nylon thread
- 3/8" wide dotted ribbon
- 1 1/8" diameter button

Here's a fabulous way to liven up the kitchen! Match right sides and use a 1/4" seam allowance for all sewing unless otherwise noted.

For the pot holder front, use the **rotary cutter** to cut an 18"-long strip from each fabric scrap, making each strip narrower on one end, but at least 1 1/2" wide (Fig. 1).

Fig. 1

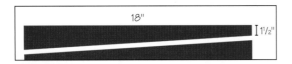

Match the long edges and sew the strips together, alternating the wide and narrow ends. Press all the seams in one direction. Cut an 8 1/2" square from the pieced strips for the pot holder front (we cut ours on the diagonal). Cut a same-size piece from backing fabric and an 8" square from batting.

Center and pin the batting on the wrong side of the pot holder front. Zigzag the front to the batting along the seams using nylon thread.

Leaving an opening for turning, sew the front and back together. **Trim the corners,** turn right side out and press. Sew the opening closed.

Fold a 7" ribbon length in half and sew the button and ribbon ends to one corner of the pot holder.

Use the leftover pieced scraps and make coasters the same way (we cut 5" squares to make our coasters).

SLING BAG
Basic Instructions, *pages 36-39*
(also shown on page 13)

- 7/8 yard fabric for bag
- 7/8 yard coordinating fabric for lining
- 3 7/8 yards rickrack
- two 1 1/2" diameter self-covered buttons

This stylish bag makes a great catchall. Cut two 16"x30" pieces each from the bag and lining fabrics. Matching right sides, pin, then use a 1/2" seam allowance to sew the bag pieces together on all four sides. Cut the rectangle on the diagonal from one corner to the opposite corner. Repeat with the lining pieces.

Turn each triangular bag piece right side out. Pin rickrack along the open diagonal edges. Sew in place along the center of the rickrack (Fig. 1).

Insert a bag piece in a lining piece. Pin the bag and lining together along the diagonal edges. Leaving an opening near the bottom for turning, sew the bag piece to the lining along the previously stitched line. Turn right side out and press. **Topstitch** along the diagonal edges using a narrow zigzag stitch.

Slip one lined bag piece inside the other, overlapping all but 3" of one bottom corner (Fig. 2). Matching the bottom seams, pin, then sew along the bottom seam through all layers.

Fig. 1

Fig. 2

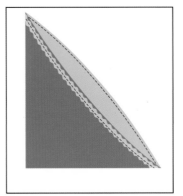
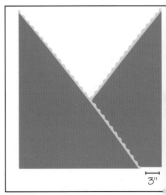

Working with the bag front only, pin the front pieces together along the overlapping diagonal edges. Refer to Fig. 3 and sew the front pieces, leaving a 6" pocket opening where shown.

Working with the bag back only, follow Fig. 4 to sew along the outer diagonal edge only (this will make a large triangular inside pocket).

Fig. 3   **Fig. 4**

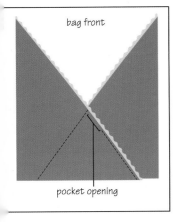 

bag front

pocket opening

bag back

Overlap the top points of the bag by 2" and sew hem together with a few machine stitches.

Cover the buttons with the lining fabric. Sew one utton to the top of the bag and one to the front bove the pocket.

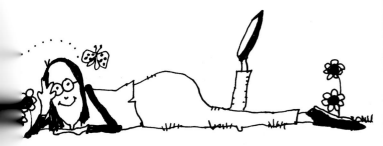

COVERED HANGERS
Basic Instructions, *pages 36-39*
(also shown on page 9)

For each cover, you will need:
- 17" wide clothes hanger
- kraft paper
- $1/4$ yard fabric for cover
- $1/8$ yard fabric for flat fabric trim or $1/3$ yard fabric for pleated trim
- $1^1/8$ yards of $1^1/2$" wide lace trim and fabric glue or 1" wide ribbon
- $3/8$" wide velveteen ribbon

With today's variety of fun fabrics to choose from, you won't be able to stop with one or two covers! Match right sides and use a $1/4$" seam allowance for all sewing unless otherwise noted.

It's simple to make a custom pattern for your hanger cover. Draw around the hanger (excluding the hook) on kraft paper, adding $1/2$" to the top and sides Draw a straight line across the bottom, 1" below the bottom of the hanger. Using the pattern, cut a front and back from cover fabric.

For the hanger with the flat fabric trim, measure across the bottom of the pattern and cut two $4^1/2$" wide fabric strips this length. Sew a strip to the bottom of each cover piece; press the seam allowanc toward the strip. Leaving $1/4$" at the center top open for the hook, sew the cover front and back together along the top and sides. Press the bottom edge $1/4$", then $1^3/4$" to the wrong side. Sew near the pressed ed turn right side out. Glue lace around the hanger cove covering the seams.

For the hanger with the pleated trim, cut two 5"x40" fabric strips. Matching wrong sides and long edges, fold each fabric strip in half; press. **Pleat** each strip. Matching raw edges and using a $1/2$" seam allowance, sew the basted trim to the bottom of eac cover piece; cut away the excess pleated trim. Press the seam allowances toward the cover. **Topstitch** 1" wide ribbon to each cover piece, covering the seam. Leaving $1/4$" at the center top open for the hook, sew t cover front and back together along the top and side turn right side out.

For each cover, sew a $3/8$" ribbon bow to the top of the cover.

CRAWSTRING BAG

Basic Instructions, pages 36-39
Pattern, page 33
(also shown on page 11)

- Tea towel
- 30" length of 1/2" wide twill tape
- Safety pin
- Tracing paper
- Two felt scraps
- Two 1/2" diameter buttons

A darling bag to give as a gift...better make an extra to keep for yourself. Keep the length of the towel (ours is 28" long) and trim it to 8 1/2" wide. Matching the right sides and short ends, fold the trimmed towel in half.

Leaving a 1" opening 2 3/4" from the top on one side, use a 1/2" seam allowance and sew the sides of the bag together. **Trim the corners** and press the seam allowances open. Press the top edge 2" to the wrong side. Sew around the top of the bag 2", 3/4" and 3/8" from the top to form the casing. Turn the bag right side out.

Fold one end of the twill tape and pin with the safety pin. Insert the pin end of the tape in the opening at the side seam. Run the tape through the casing and remove the pin. Using the pattern, cut two flowers from felt. Sew a flower and button near each end of the tape.

RIBBIT

Basic Instructions, pages 36-39
Patterns, pages 33-35
(also shown on page 23)

- tracing paper
- 1/2 yard wool felt
- fabric scraps
- pinking shears
- liquid fray preventative
- embroidery floss
- doll-stuffing pellets or lentils
- polyester fiberfill

This lovable sit-about will look great wherever he lands because he's filled with stuffing pellets that help him hold his pose. Match right sides and use a 1/4" seam allowance for all sewing unless otherwise noted.

Using the patterns, cut two frog shapes from wool felt and the eye circles from fabric scraps. Use pinking shears to cut the remaining shapes from fabric scraps. Apply fray preventative to the edges of each fabric shape and allow to dry.

Pin, then sew the eyes and circles to the frog back piece about 1/8" inside the raw edges of the circles. Using six strands of floss, add **French knot** cheeks.

On the frog front, avoiding the seam allowances, sew the shapes in place 1/8" inside the edges of the toe- and footpads, and 1/4" inside the belly edges.

Matching the right sides, sew the frog front and back together, leaving an opening for turning at the crotch. Turn right side out and pour pellets into the head and front legs. Stuff the chest with fiberfill and add pellets to the back legs and stomach. Sew the opening closed.

Patterns

Napkins, page 3

Sunflower Pillow, page 6

Girl's Receiving Blanket, page 21
and
Appliquéd Baby Blanket, page 22

Leisure Arts, Inc., grants
permission to the owner of this
book to photocopy the patterns on
this page for personal use only.

Strip-Pieced Pillow, page 8

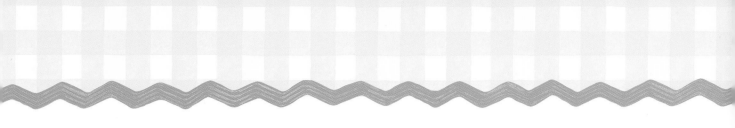

Boy's Receiving Blanket, page 20

Appliquéd Baby Blanket,
page 22

Gift Bags, page 10

Appliquéd Baby Blanket,
page 22

Drawstring Bag, page 27

Leisure Arts, Inc., grants permission to the owner
of this book to photocopy the patterns on this
page for personal use only.

Ribbit, page 28

toepad (cut 6)

eye (cut 2)

footpad (cut 2)

back (cut 8)

belly

Ribbit, page 28

Leisure Arts, Inc., grants permission to the owner of this book to
photocopy the pattern on this page for personal use only.

Basic Instructions

For your convenience, we highlighted topics in the project instructions that are explained in more detail the following pages. There are all kinds of projects you can sew using these simple tips and techniques!

SEWING BASICS

APPLIQUÉ
Backed with Fusible Web

We recommend this technique for projects that require frequent washing. Cut a piece of paper-backed fusible web a little larger than the pattern (about an inch or so on each side). Trace the pattern onto tracing paper. Turn the traced pattern over and trace this reversed pattern onto the paper side of the web. Cut about 1/2" outside the pattern lines. Iron the web to the wrong side of the fabric (Fig. 1). (When working with multiple patterns to be cut from one piece of fabric, cut a piece of fusible web slightly smaller than the fabric piece. Trace the reversed pattern as many times as you wish onto the paper side of the web and iron the web to the wrong side of the fabric piece.) Cut out the shape(s).

Remove the paper backing and fuse the appliqué to the background fabric (Fig. 2). Zigzag around the edges of the appliqué with clear nylon thread or you may wish to choose a contrasting thread color.

Fig. 1

Fig. 2

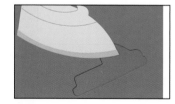

Non-Backed for Soft, Frayed Edges

For projects that won't need to be washed very often, use this method for a softer, more primitive look. Trace the pattern onto tracing paper and cut the shape from fabric. Pin, then sew the appliqué to the background fabric, about 1/4" inside the raw edges (Fig. 1).

Fig. 1

HEMMING

It's easy to make a straight hem using a hem gauge. Use a purchased gauge or make your own and press the edge to be hemmed to the wrong side.

To make a gauge, draw a line 1/4" (or the amount given in the project instructions) from the edge of a strip of thin cardboard. Place the strip near the raw edge of the fabric, fold the fab edge around the strip to meet the line and press (Fig. 1). Move the strip along the length of the fabric until the whole edge is pressed.

Where instructions say to fold the raw edge to the wrong side twice, fold pressed edge to the wrong side and pr (Fig. 2). Pin in place. Topstitch or hand sew along the pressed edge, removing pins as you come to them.

Fig. 1

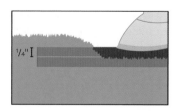

Fig. 2

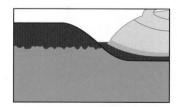

MATCHING INTERSECTIONS

For intersections that match up and look great, it's important to begin by sewing accurate seams as you sew the pieces together for each row. Press the seams on the first row to the right, the second row to the left and the third to the right (Fig. 1). Pin the first two rows right sides together, being careful to match the seams. Sew and repeat for the last two rows.

Fig. 1

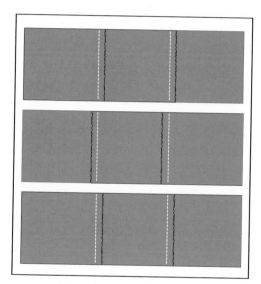

MITERING CORNERS
Background Fabric

To miter the corners of a piece of fabric, first press the seam allowances on all sides and unfold. Press the corners diagonally across the pressed point, then trim (Fig. 1). Refold and press the sides (Fig. 2). Follow the project instructions to cover the raw edges with trim.

Fig. 1

Fig. 2

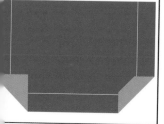
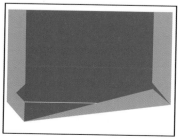

Trim

Covering the raw fabric edges, pin the trim up to the mitered corner of the background fabric (Fig. 1). Fold the trim back on itself and insert a pin diagonally at the corner through all layers (Fig. 2). Follow Fig. 3 to fold the mitered corner. Continue pinning and folding in this way until you reach the beginning of the trim. Overlapping the tape ends, fold the top end under 1/2" (cut off the excess) and pin in place. Topstitch along the long edges of the trim.

Fig. 1

Fig. 2

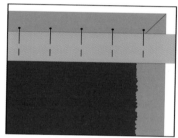
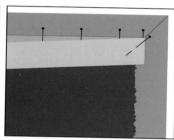

Fig. 3

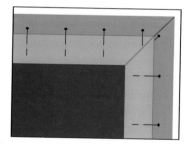

PLEATING

Working along the long raw edges, use a pin to mark 1" from one end. Follow Fig. 1 to measure and alternately mark ¼", then 1" until you reach the end of the strip.

Follow Fig. 2 to accordion fold the pleats. Pin, then press the pleats, and baste along the raw edges.

Fig. 1

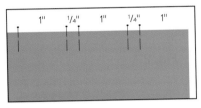

Fig. 2

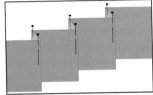

ROTARY CUTTING

For safety, look for a cutter with a blade that stays closed until you push down to cut. If your cutter has a manual retractable blade, immediately close the blade after each cut. Use a cutting mat to protect your surface. Hold the ruler firmly in place on top of the fabric with your fingers away from the edges. You may wish to use a Klutz Glove™. This is a cut-resistant glove to wear on the hand that holds the ruler to prevent injury. Always cut in a direction away from your body.

Line up the fabric with a vertical line on the cutting mat. Using the measurements on the ruler, line up the ruler over the fabric where you need to make your cut. Hold the cutter at an angle with the blade against the edge of the ruler and cut the fabric (Fig. 1).

Fig. 1

TOPSTITCHING

Topstitching is a line of stitching close to a seam or the edge of a project, that accentuates the seam line or edge (Fig. 1).

Fig. 1

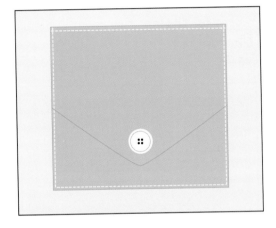

TRIM THE CORNERS

Follow the project instructions to sew two fabric pieces together. Before turning right side out, trim the corners as shown to keep them from becoming bulky (Fig. 1).

Fig. 1

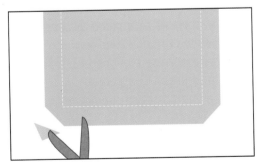

YO-YOS

To make each yo-yo, cut a circle the size given in the project instructions. Press the circle edge 1/8" to the wrong side and sew **Running Stitches** around the edge with a doubled strand of thread. Pull the thread tightly to gather. Knot and trim the thread. Move the small opening to the center of the circle.

Fig. 1

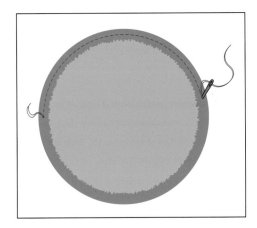

MAKING PATTERNS
TWO-PART PATTERNS

When tracing a two-part pattern, match the dashed lines to trace the patterns onto tracing paper, forming a whole pattern.

EMBROIDERY

Use 3 strands of embroidery floss for all stitches unless otherwise indicated in project instructions. Follow the stitch diagrams to bring the needle up at odd numbers and down at even numbers.

FRENCH KNOT

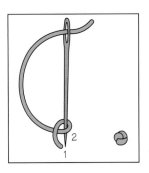

RUNNING STITCH

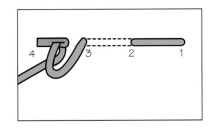

STRAIGHT STITCH

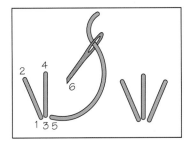

Credits

Designers: Becky Werle, Kim Kern, Kelly Reider,
Anne Pulliam Stocks and Lori Wenger
Editorial Writer: Susan McManus Johnson
Project Writer: Laura Siar Holyfield
Graphic Artist: Angela Ormsby Stark
Photo Stylist: Christy Myers

We want to extend a warm thank you to
The DMC Corporation for providing the embroidery floss used in this book.